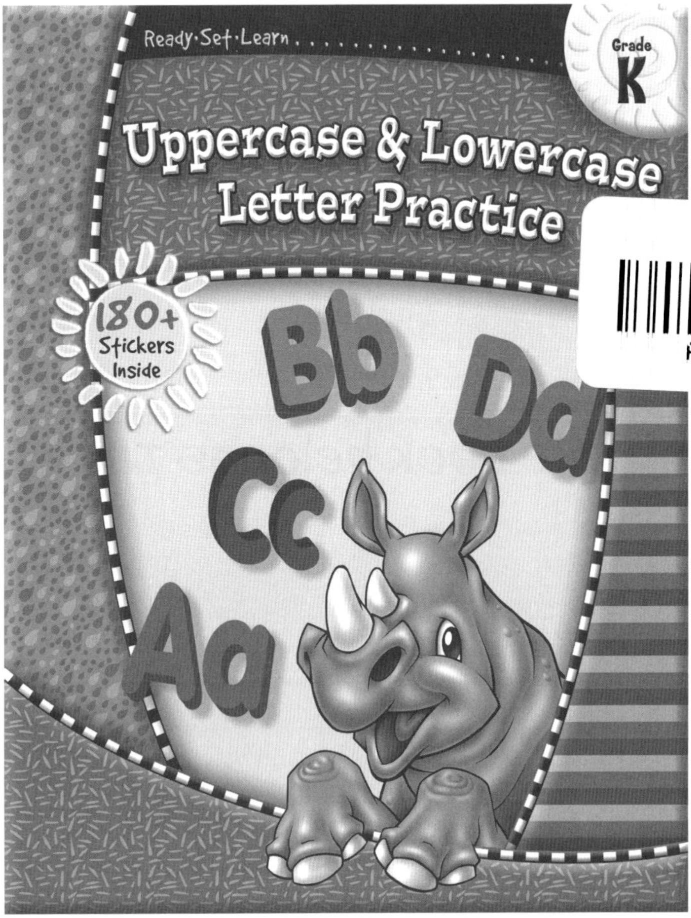

Managing Editor
Ina Massler Levin, M.A.

Editor
Eric Migliaccio

Contributing Editors
Sarah Smith
Kristine Smith

Creative Director
Karen J. Goldfluss, M.S. Ed.

Cover Design
Tony Carrillo / Marilyn Goldberg

Teacher Created Resources
12621 Western Avenue
Garden Grove, CA 92841
www.teachercreated.com

ISBN: 978-1-4206-5973-3

©2007 Teacher Created Resources
Reprinted, 2023 (PO604631)

Made in U.S.A.

The material in this book is intended for individual use only. No part of this publication may be transmitted, reproduced, stored, or recorded in any form without written permission from the publisher.

This book belongs to

_____

Ready·Set·Learn

Get Ready to Learn!

Get ready, get set, and go! Boost your child's learning with this exciting series of books. Geared to help children practice and master many needed skills, the *Ready·Set·Learn* books are bursting with 64 pages of learning fun. Use these books for . . .

 enrichment   skills reinforcement   extra practice

With their smaller size, the *Ready·Set·Learn* books fit easily in children's hands, backpacks, and book bags. All your child needs to get started are pencils, crayons, and colored pencils.

A full sheet of colorful stickers is included. Use these stickers for . . .

- decorating pages
- rewarding outstanding effort
- keeping track of completed pages

Celebrate your child's progress by using these stickers on the reward chart located on the inside cover. The blue-ribbon sticker fits perfectly on the certificate on page 64.

With *Ready·Set·Learn* and a little encouragement, your child will be on the fast track to learning fun!

Trace the Letters

Directions: Trace over the shaded guide to form the uppercase and lowercase letters.

Aa Bb Cc

Aa	Bb	Cc
Dd	Ee	Ff
Gg	Hh	Ii
Jj	Kk	Ll

Lowercase Letters

Directions: Trace over the shaded guide to form the uppercase and lowercase letters.

	Mm	Nn
Oo	Pp	Qq
Rr	Ss	Tt
Uu	Vv	Ww
Xx	Yy	Zz

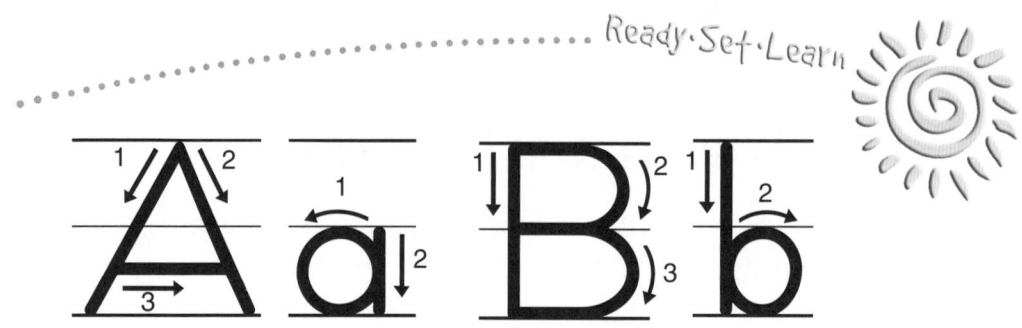

Directions: Trace each uppercase and lowercase letter. Write each letter as many times as you can.

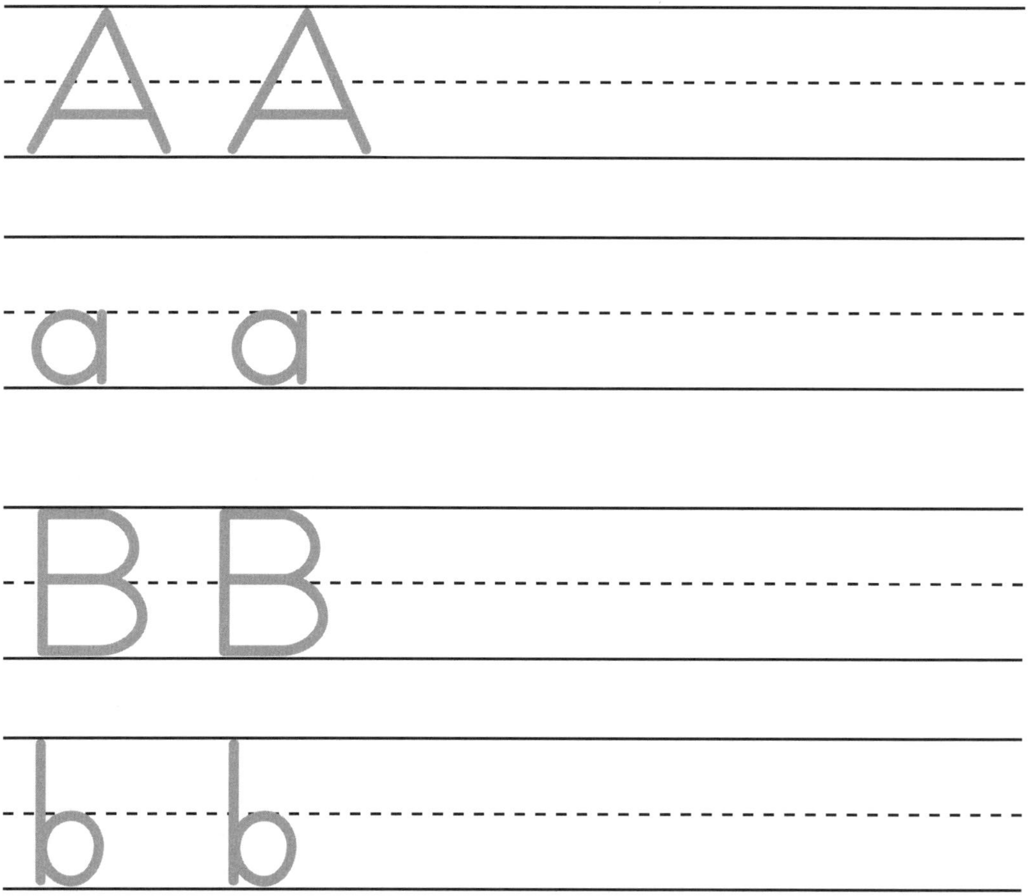

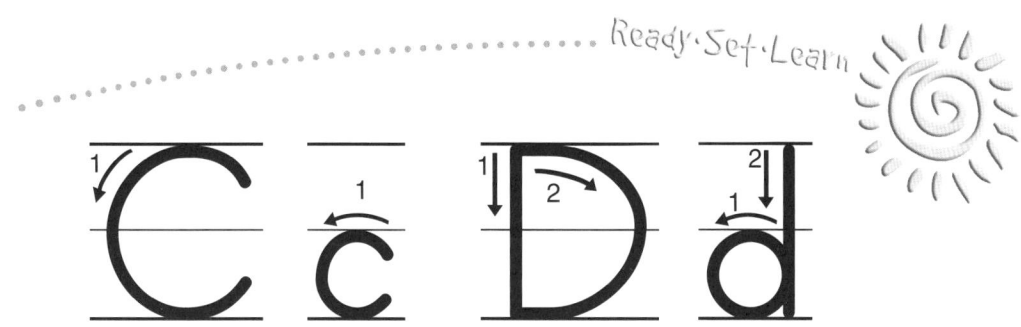

Directions: Trace each uppercase and lowercase letter. Write each letter as many times as you can.

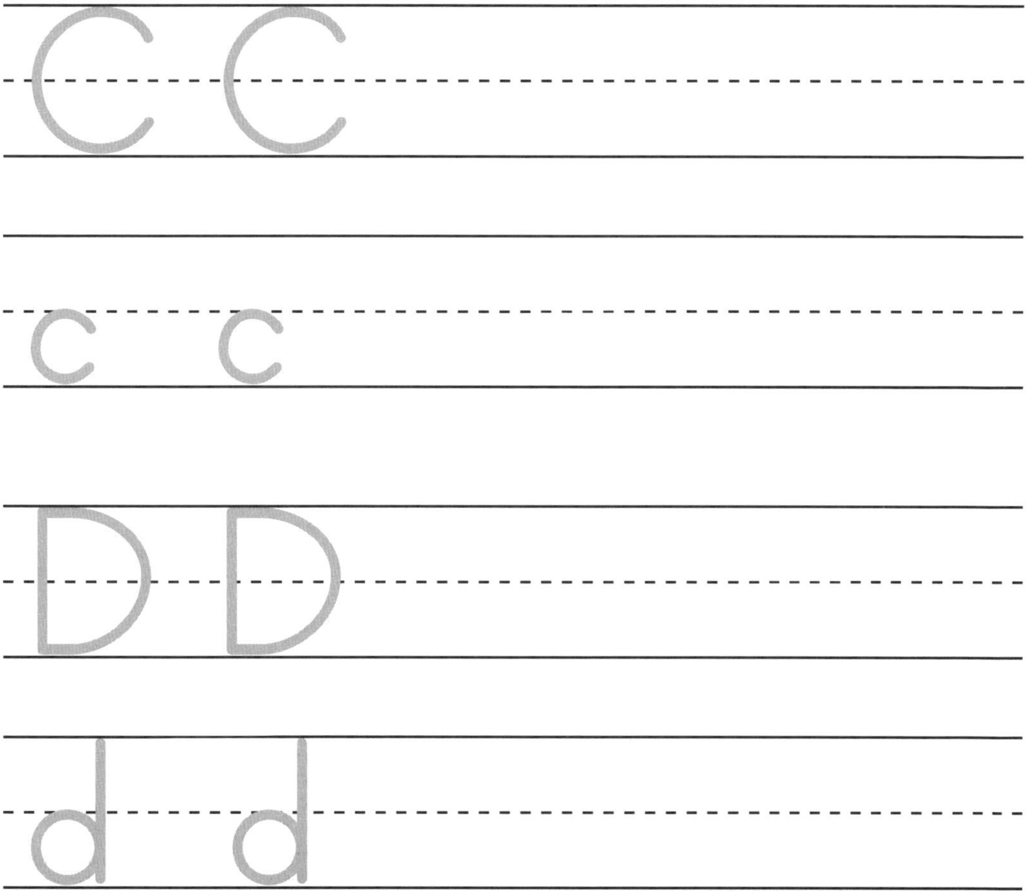

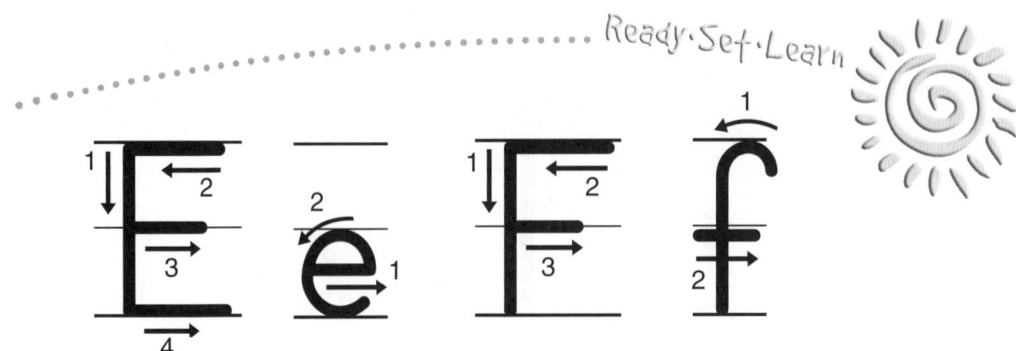

Directions: Trace each uppercase and lowercase letter. Write each letter as many times as you can.

E E

F F e e

f f

 ©Teacher Created Resources, Inc.

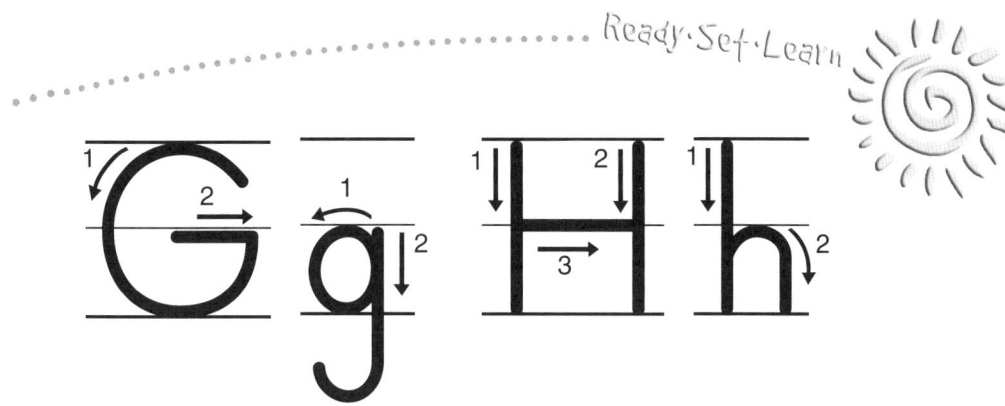

Directions: Trace each uppercase and lowercase letter. Write each letter as many times as you can.

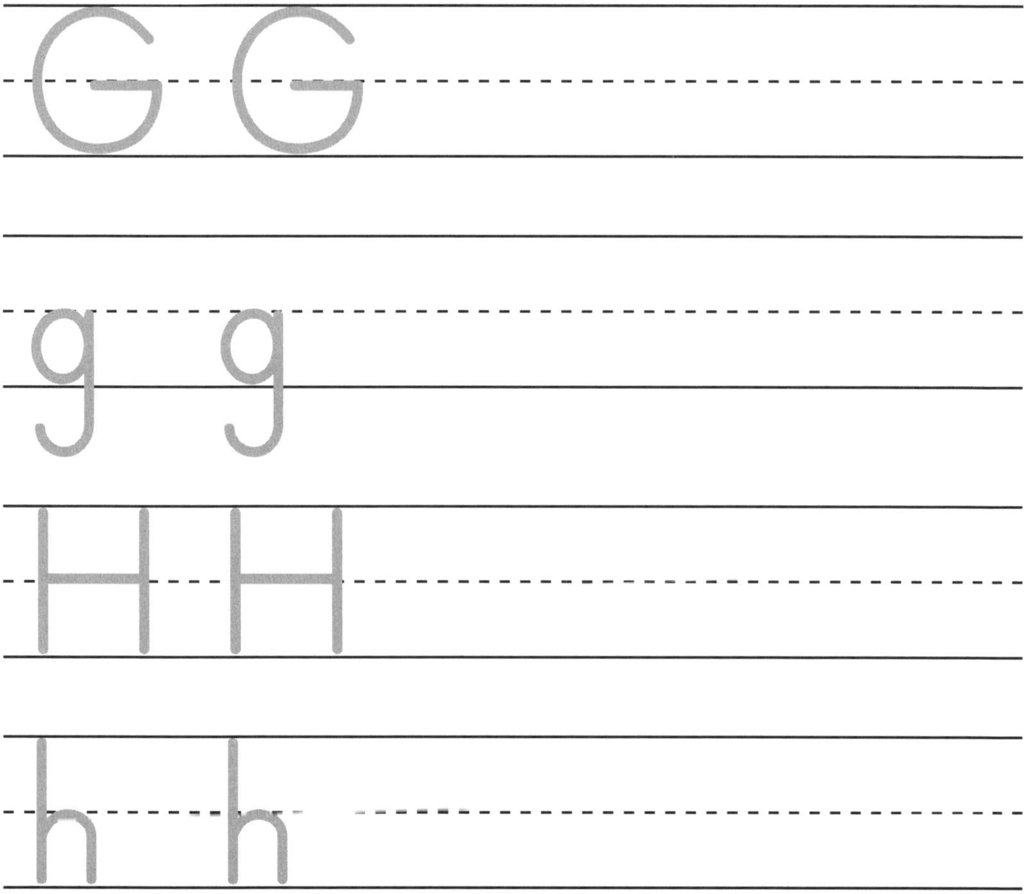

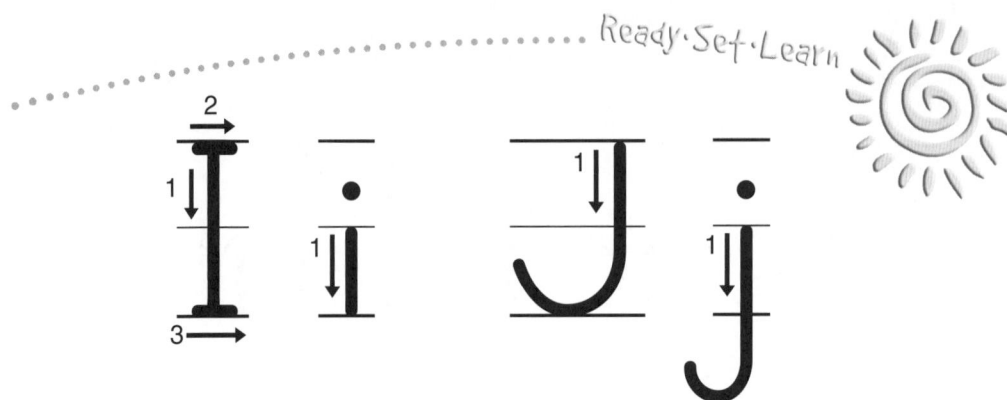

Directions: Trace each uppercase and lowercase letter. Write each letter as many times as you can.

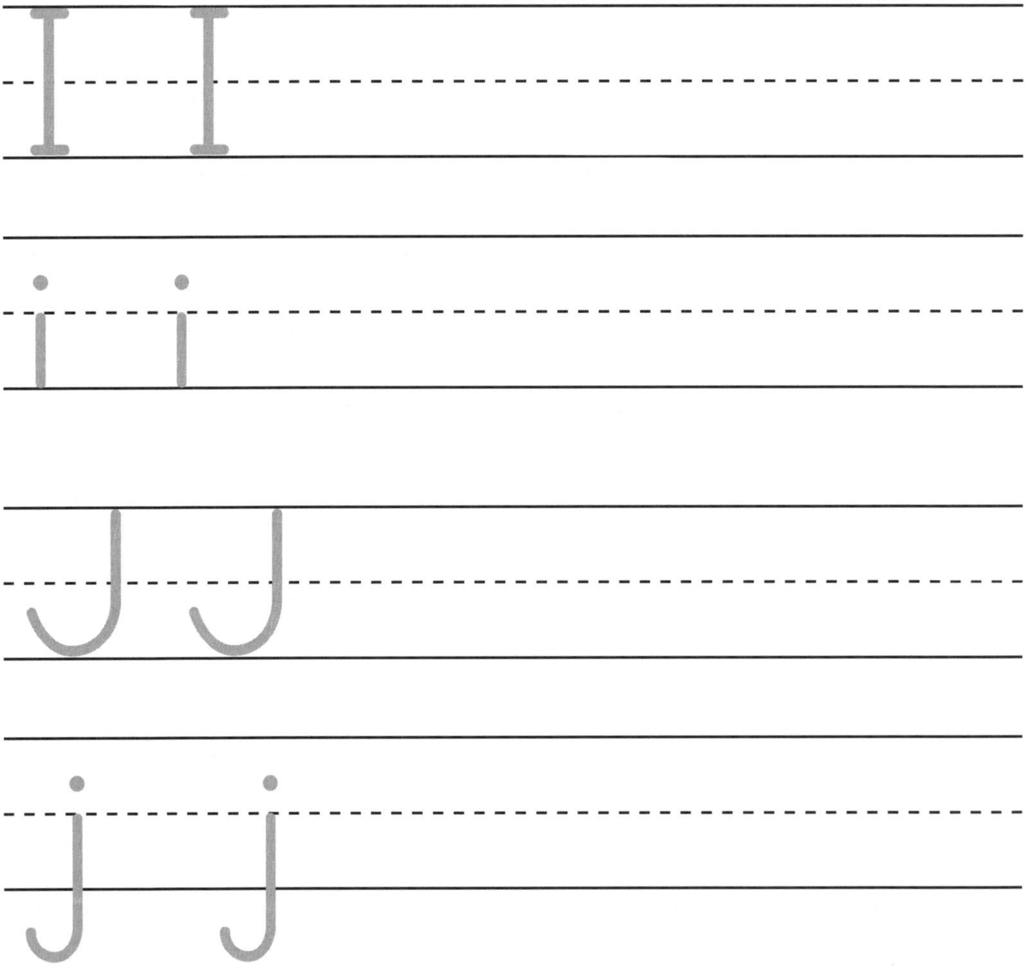

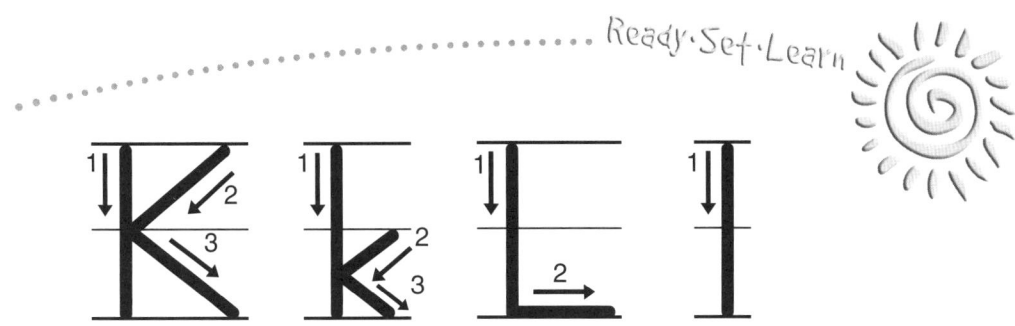

Directions: Trace each uppercase and lowercase letter. Write each letter as many times as you can.

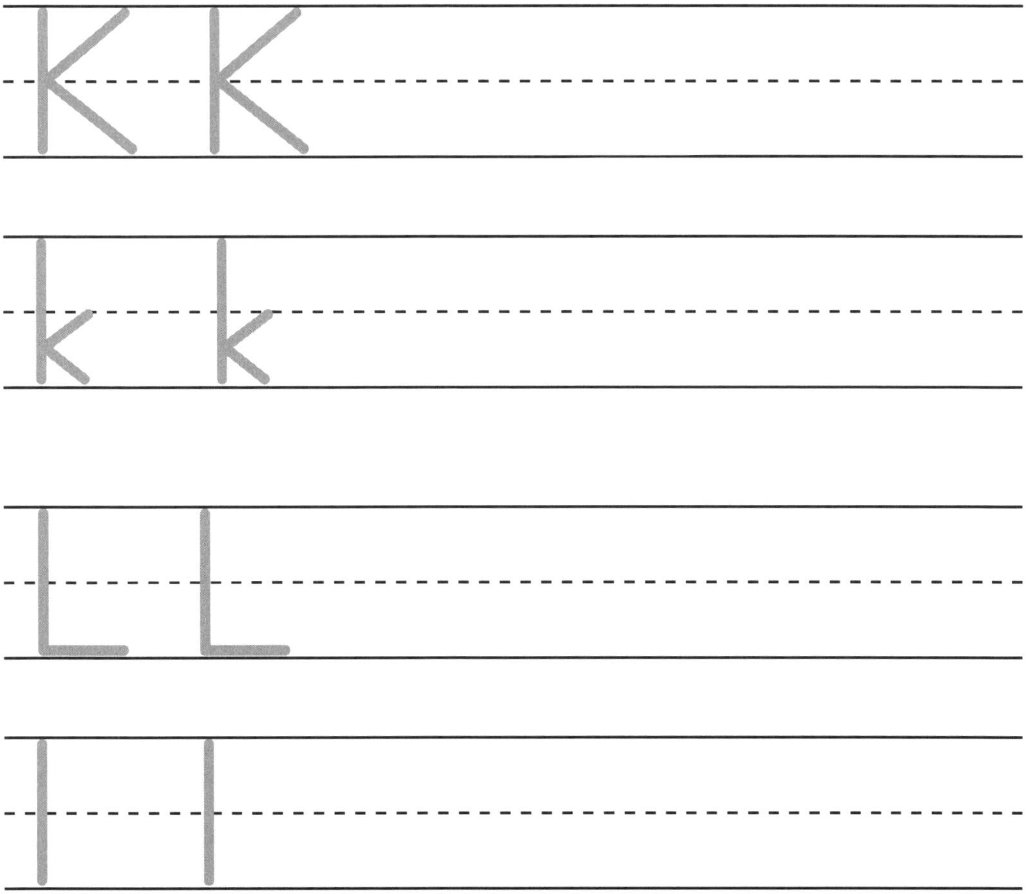

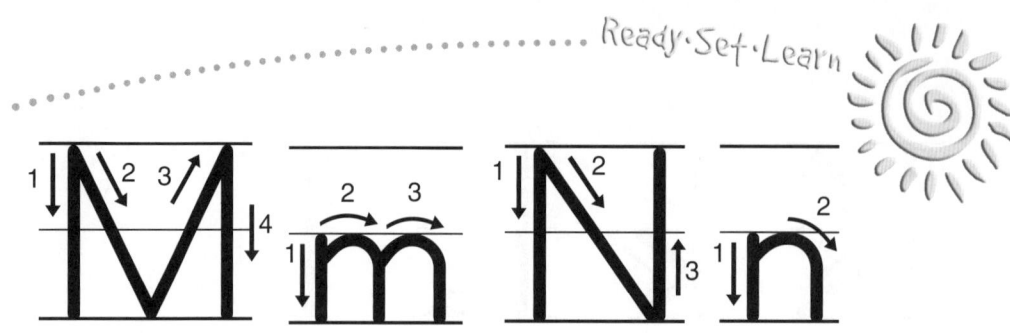

Directions: Trace each uppercase and lowercase letter. Write each letter as many times as you can.

M M

m m

N N

n n

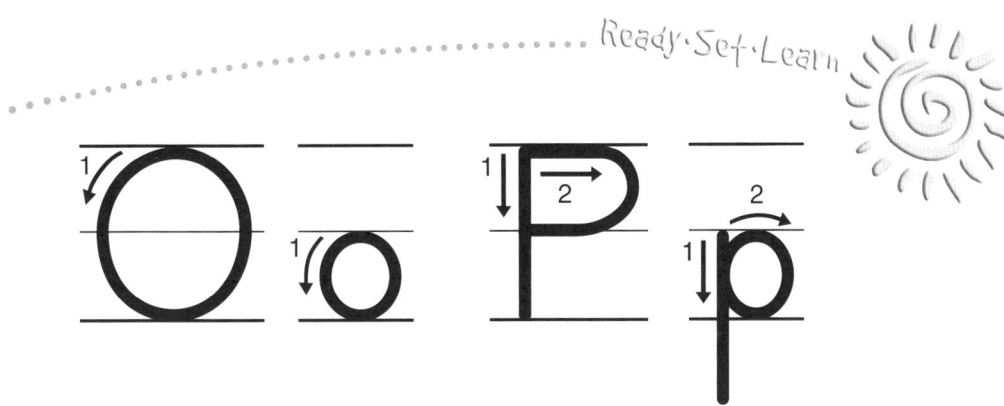

Directions: Trace each uppercase and lowercase letter. Write each letter as many times as you can.

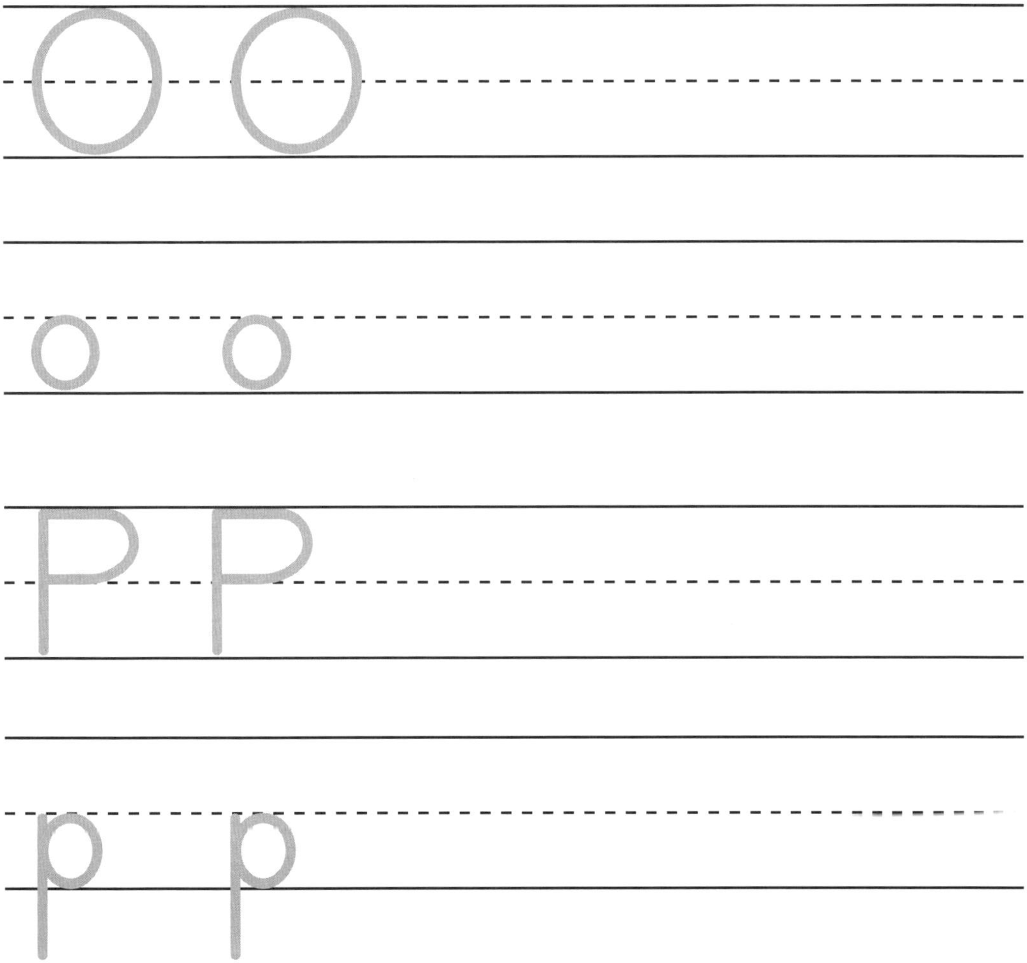

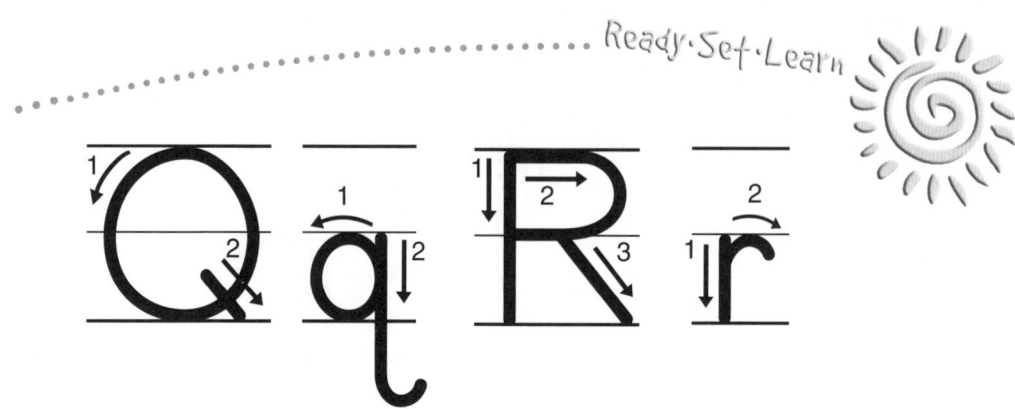

Directions: Trace each uppercase and lowercase letter. Write each letter as many times as you can.

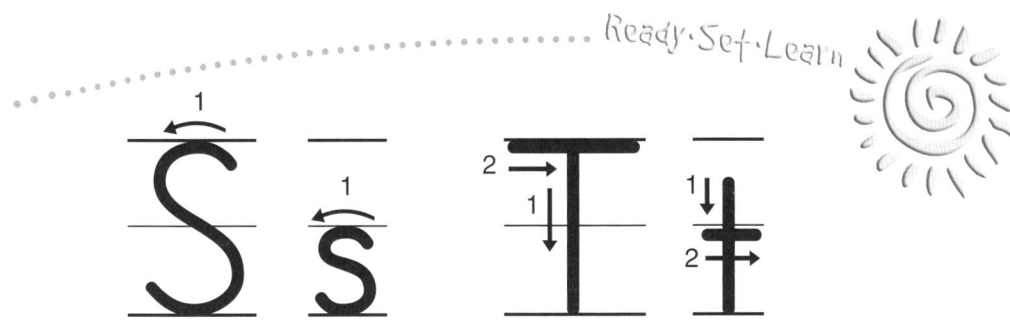

Directions: Trace each uppercase and lowercase letter. Write each letter as many times as you can.

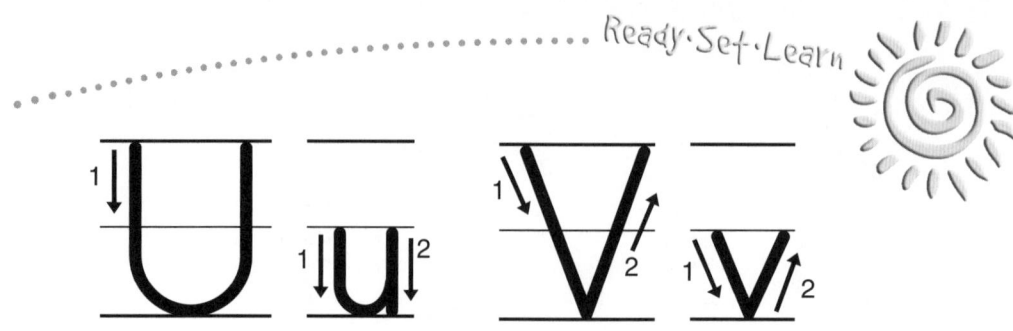

Directions: Trace each uppercase and lowercase letter. Write each letter as many times as you can.

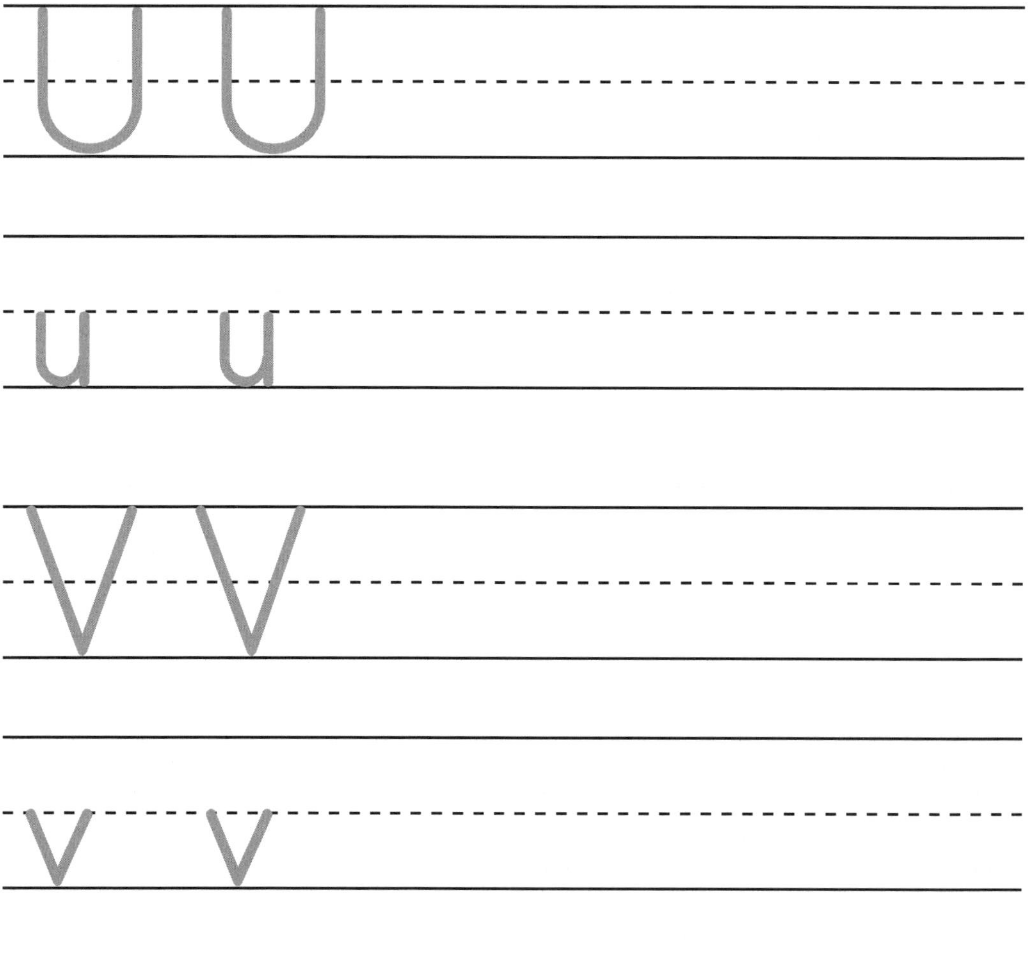

Ready·Set·Learn

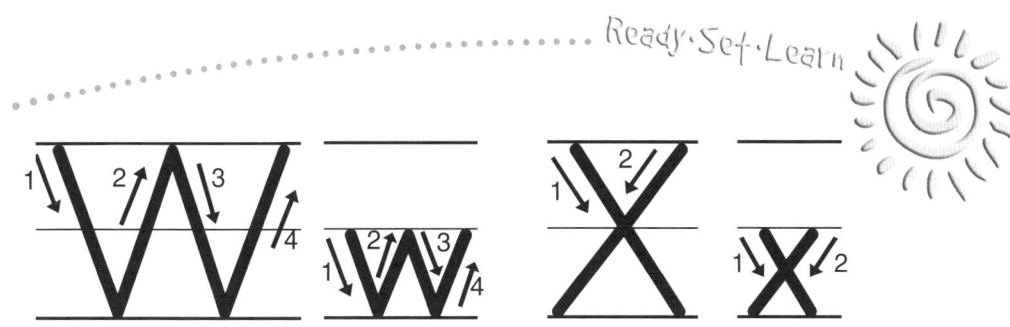

Directions: Trace each uppercase and lowercase letter. Write each letter as many times as you can.

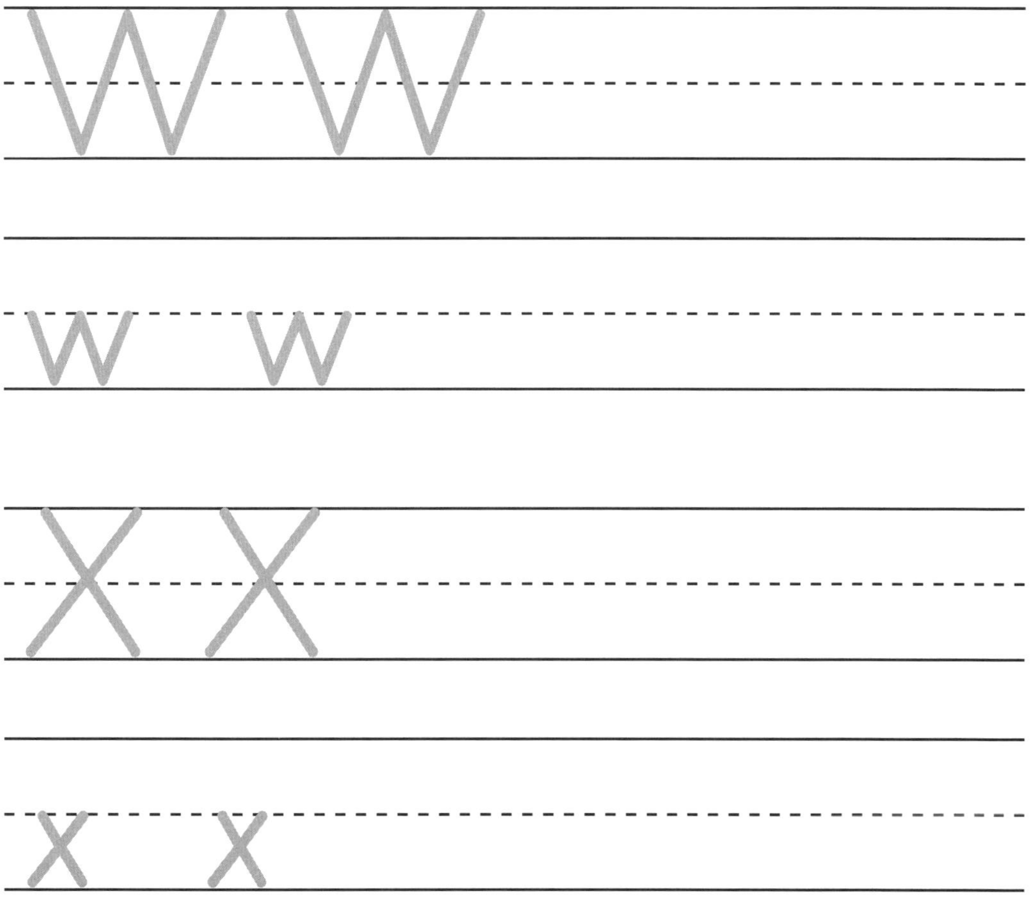

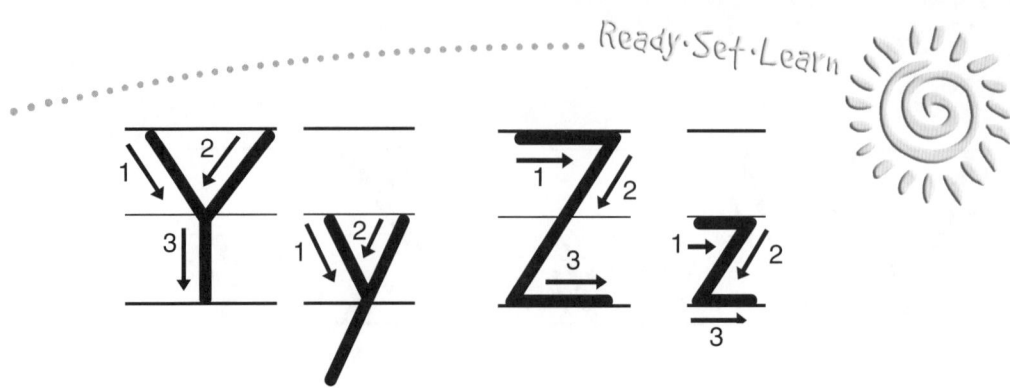

Directions: Trace each uppercase and lowercase letter. Write each letter as many times as you can.

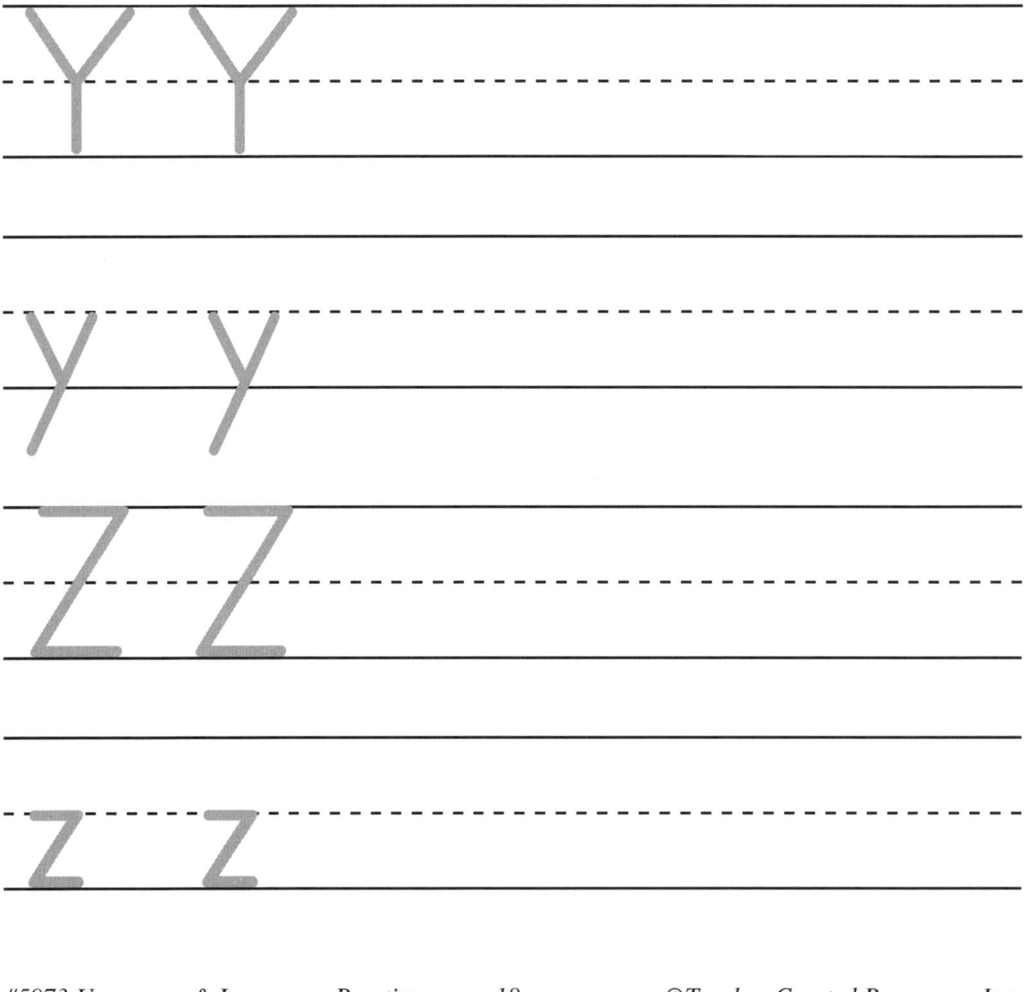

I Can Print the Alphabet

Directions: Trace the letters of the alphabet.

A B C D

E F G H

I J K L

M N O P

Q R S T

U V W X

Y Z

Lowercase Letter Match

Directions: Write the matching lowercase letter next to each uppercase letter.

A _ _ _ _   B _ _ _ _   C _ _ _ _   D _ _ _ _

E _ _ _ _   F _ _ _ _   G _ _ _ _   H _ _ _ _

I _ _ _ _   J _ _ _ _   K _ _ _ _   L _ _ _ _

M _ _ _ _   N _ _ _ _   O _ _ _ _   P _ _ _ _

Q _ _ _ _   R _ _ _ _   S _ _ _ _   T _ _ _ _

U _ _ _ _   V _ _ _ _   W _ _ _ _   X _ _ _ _

Y _ _ _ _   Z _ _ _ _

Uppercase Letter Match

Directions: Write the matching uppercase letter next to each lowercase letter.

a _____   b _____   c _____   d _____

e _____   f _____   g _____   h _____

i _____   j _____   k _____   l _____

m _____   n _____   o _____   p _____

q _____   r _____   s _____   t _____

u _____   v _____   w _____   x _____

y _____   z _____

Alphabet Train

Directions: Fill in the missing uppercase letters of the alphabet.

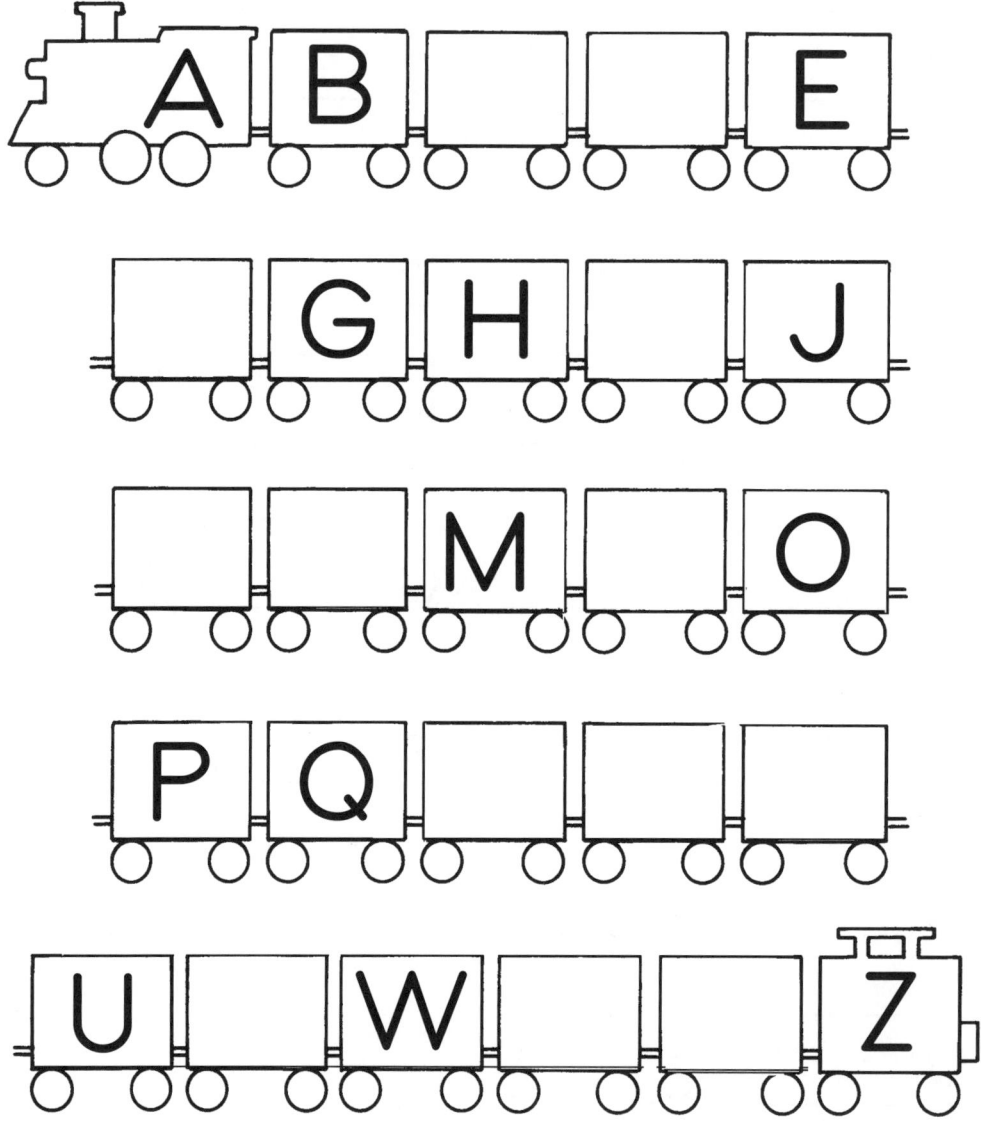

Alpha-Bug

Directions: Fill in the missing lowercase letters of the alphabet.

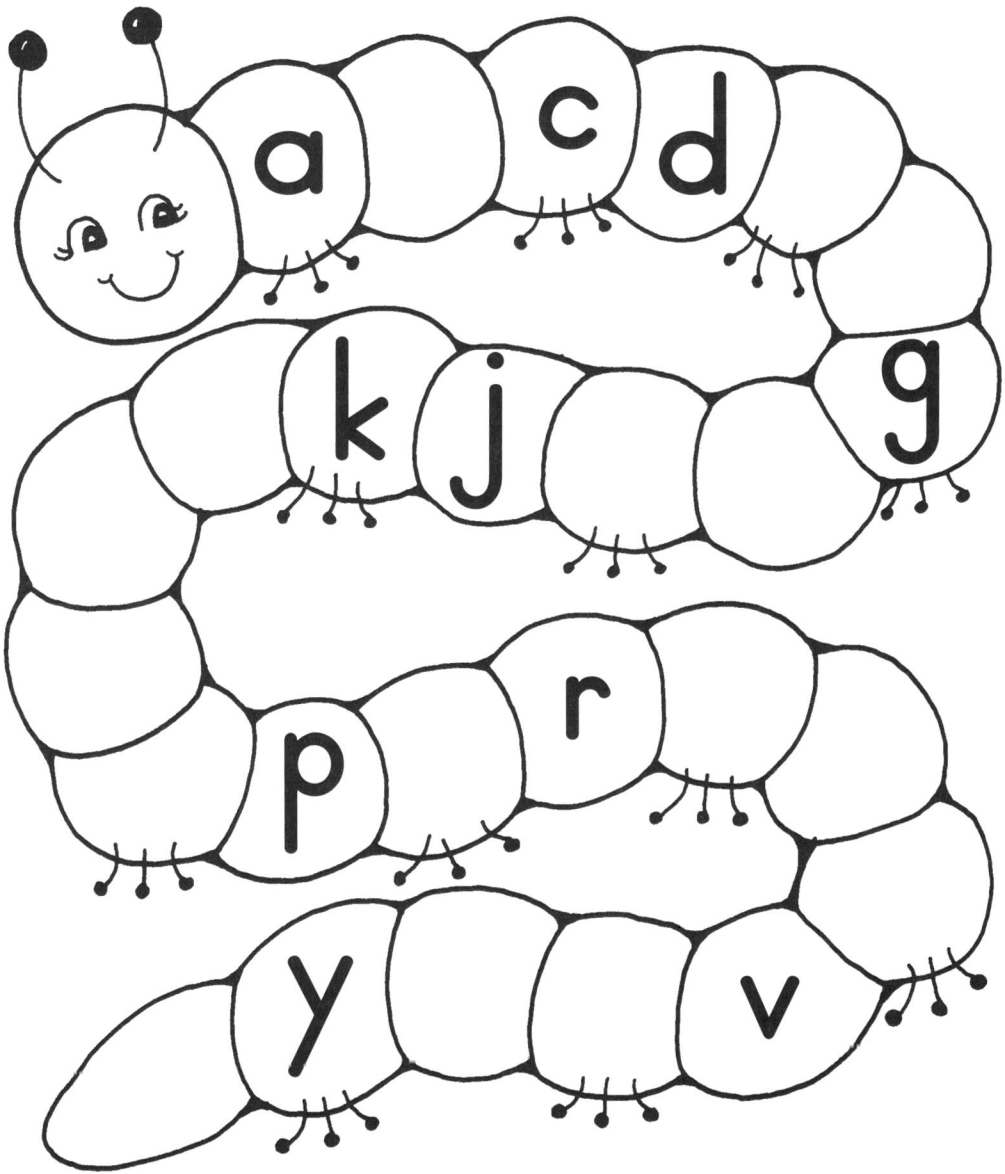

Lowercase Practice (A–D)

Directions: Circle the matching lowercase letter.

A	F	B	a	A
B	b	X	B	D
C	o	C	c	Q
D	O	g	D	d

Lowercase Practice (E–H)

Directions: Circle the matching lowercase letter.

E	e H f E
F	f g F T
G	G y g Q
H	W H R h

Ready·Set·Learn

Lowercase Practice (I–L)

Directions: Circle the matching lowercase letter.

I	L	I	i	j
J	j	U	p	J
K	K	R	k	m
L	f	L	I	l

Lowercase Practice (M–P)

Directions: Circle the matching lowercase letter.

M	n	m	M	N
N	n	W	N	m
O	P	q	O	o
P	b	p	R	P

Ready·Set·Learn

Lowercase Practice (Q–T)

Directions: Circle the matching lowercase letter.

Q	g q G Q
R	r B R s
S	m s S w
T	T I f t

Lowercase Practice (U–X)

Directions: Circle the matching lowercase letter.

U	n	U	O	u
V	u	X	v	V
W	w	M	W	m
X	v	x	X	M

Uppercase and Lowercase Practice

Directions: Circle the matching lowercase letter.

Y	g	Y	R	y
Z	m	z	Z	l

Directions: Circle the matching uppercase letter.

a	e	a	A	t
b	B	d	b	g

Uppercase Practice (C–F)

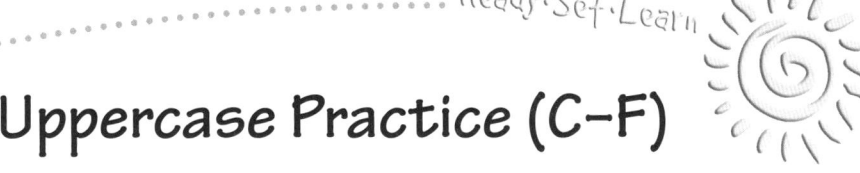

Directions: Circle the matching uppercase letter.

c	t	C	e	c
d	h	d	s	D
e	r	g	E	e
f	f	t	t	F

Uppercase Practice (G–J)

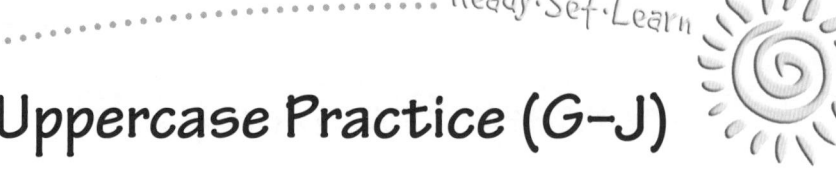

Directions: Circle the matching uppercase letter.

g	e	g	o	G
h	b	H	d	h
i	i	I	j	l
j	i	l	I	J

Uppercase Practice (K–N)

Directions: Circle the matching uppercase letter.

k	K	s	k	r
l	L	t	l	k
m	n	w	M	m
n	N	m	n	w

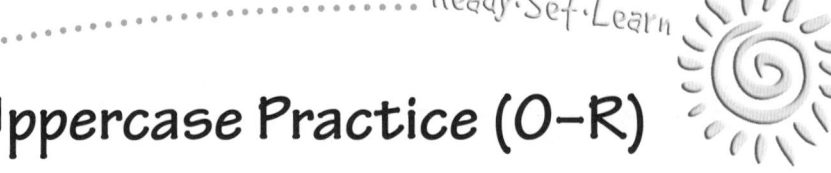

Uppercase Practice (O–R)

Directions: Circle the matching uppercase letter.

o	p O u o
p	d p g P
q	q g Q b
r	t R r o

Uppercase Practice (S-V)

Directions: Circle the matching uppercase letter.

s	S	m	g	s
t	t	g	f	T
u	n	U	u	v
v	V	w	u	v

Uppercase Practice (W–Z)

Directions: Circle the matching uppercase letter.

w	m	n	w	W
x	m	x	f	X
y	Y	v	y	m
z	z	w	Z	x

Lowercase Letter Match

Directions: Circle the letters that match in each row.

d	a	d	b	c	d	p
f	f	k	l	f	h	f	i
e	g	e	a	o	e	c
p	d	p	b	p	a	p
r	r	m	r	n	a	r
h	m	h	k	h	b	d

Ready·Set·Learn

Uppercase Letter Match

Directions: Circle the letters that match in each row.

A	L	A	M	A	W	A
H	K	L	H	Y	H	Z	T
P	B	P	D	C	P	O	L
W	W	N	X	W	Z	W
G	O	G	D	G	G	B
K	K	N	K	L	M	K	I

Mixed Case Letter Match

Directions: Circle the letters that match in each row.

M	M	Z	N	M	Y	E	N
y	z	y	k	y	y	x	i	z
Q	O	C	Q	D	S	Q	C
a	a	b	q	a	c	d	q
Z	K	Z	W	Z	M	Z
n	n	a	n	r	m	n

Matching Letters

Directions: Find the letters in each line that are the same as the letter in the box and circle them.

R	R	B	P	R	R
N	H	N	M	K	N
W	V	W	M	K	N
G	Q	G	O	C	G
P	R	S	P	P	P
C	O	D	G	C	C
Q	O	Q	D	Q	C

B is for Butterfly

Directions: Circle the letters that are the same as the beginning letter of each bug.

b is for **b**utterfly

   b d b b p d b b

a is for **a**nt

   a o o a a a e a

m is for **m**oth

   w m n m m w n m

c is for **c**aterpillar

   o c c e c e e c

©Teacher Created Resources, Inc.   #5973 Uppercase & Lowercase Practice

Ladybug Letters

Directions: Draw lines to match the uppercase and lowercase letters. Then color the ladybugs.

Match the Bubbles

Directions: Draw lines to match the uppercase letters to the lowercase letters.

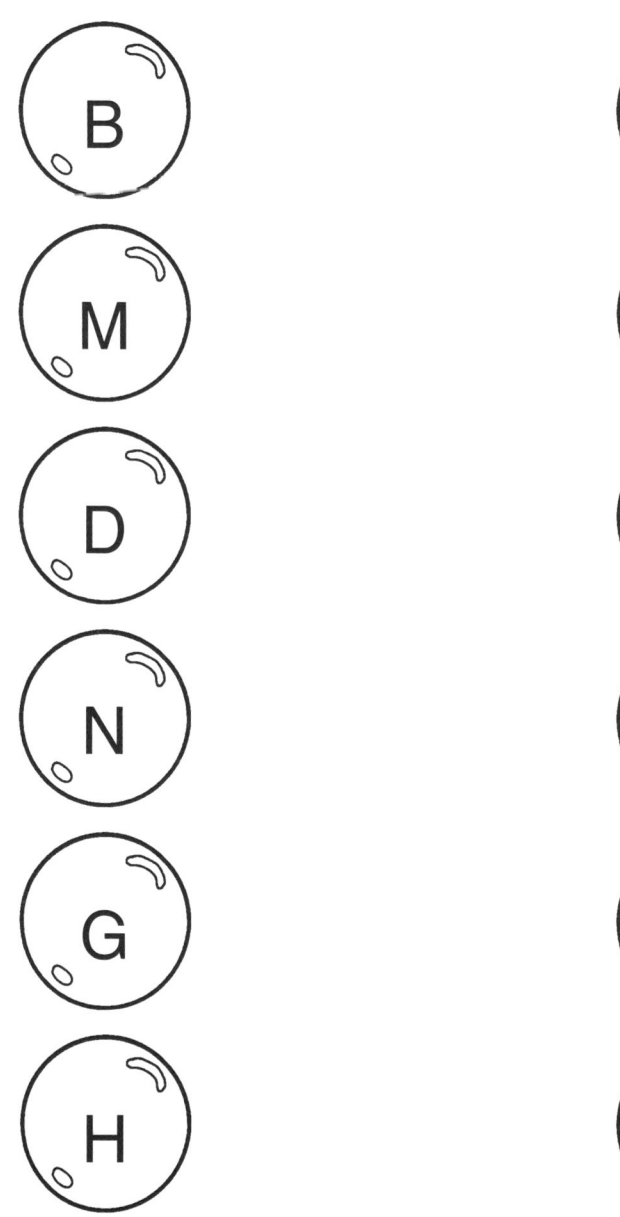

Sun Letters!

Directions: Draw lines to match the uppercase letters with the lowercase letters.

Z	t	D	f
M	b	N	r
Y	m	F	g
T	z	R	d
B	y	G	n

Letter Birds

Directions: Draw lines to match the uppercase letters on the birds with the lowercase letters on the worms.

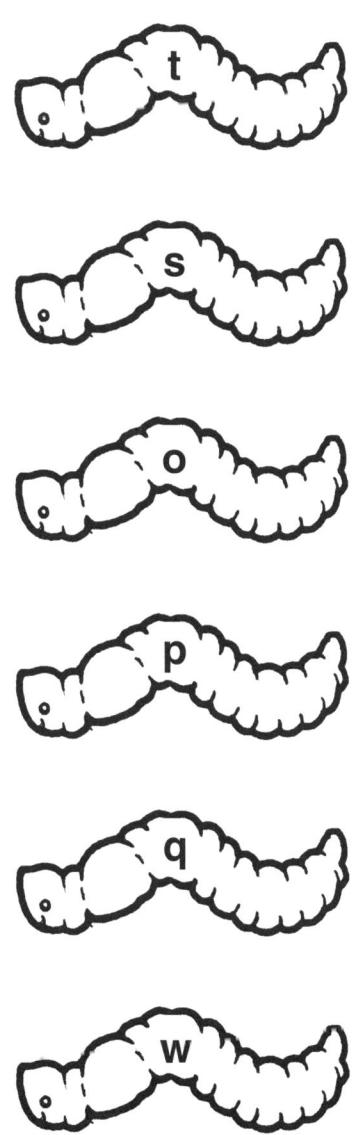

Matching Kites

Directions: Draw lines to match the uppercase letters with the lowercase letters. Then color each pair of kites.

Play Ball

Directions: Match each mitt to the ball with its partner letter. Draw a line from each uppercase letter to its lowercase partner.

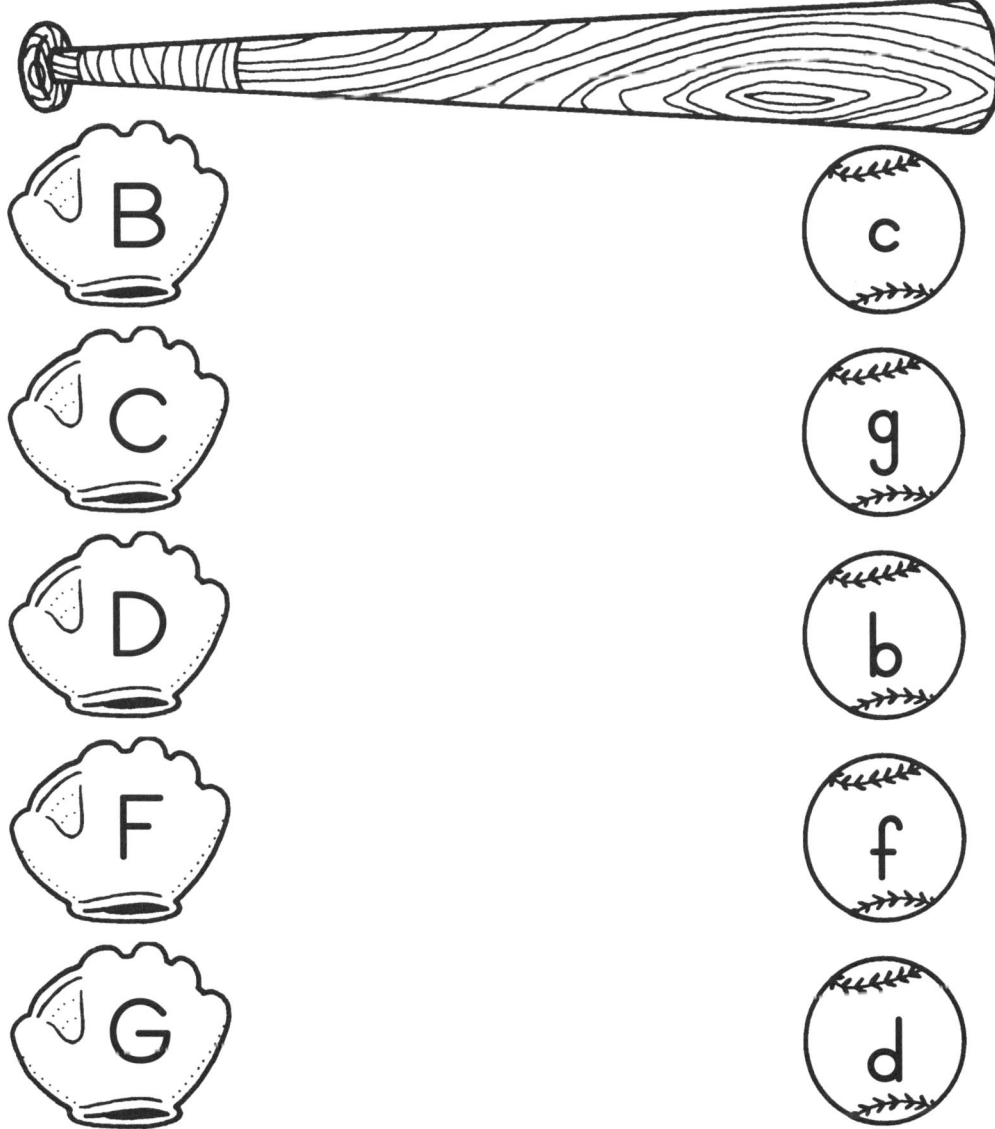

Matching Letters

Directions: Draw lines to match the uppercase and lowercase letters in each box. The first one is done for you.

A — — — c	D e
B a	E f
C b	F d

C c	F e
E b	E d
B e	D f

C d	F b
D a	E e
A c	B f

Unlock It

Directions: Unlock the door with the right key. To find the right key, match the capital letter on the door to the lowercase letter on the key. Draw a line to match them together.

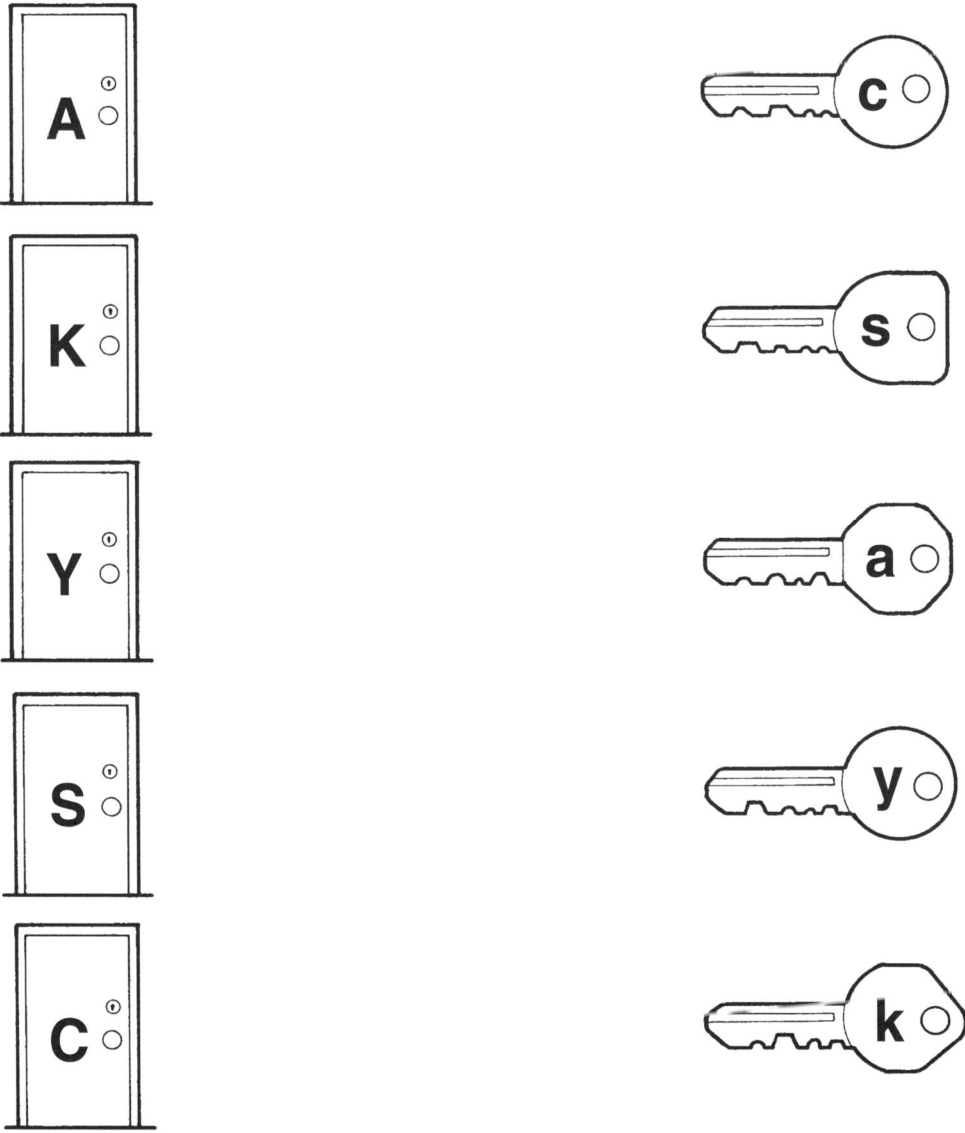

Stack and Puff Match

Directions: Draw lines to match the letter partners.

Which Stars Match?

Directions: Each uppercase consonant has a matching lowercase letter that shares the same sound. Color each star that contains a matching pair.

Ready·Set·Learn

More Matching

Directions: Draw a line from each uppercase letter to the lowercase letter that matches.

1. B   b
2. F   r
3. N   f
4. R   n

5. E   m
6. M   e
7. C   k
8. K   c

Directions: Draw a line from each uppercase letter to the lowercase letter that matches.

9. d   Y
10. y   D
11. q   Q
12. h   H

13. l   G
14. w   W
15. g   T
16. t   L

#5973 Uppercase & Lowercase Practice   ©Teacher Created Resources, Inc.

Mitten Match

Directions: Match the uppercase and lowercase letters by coloring the mittens the same color. Use a different color for each pair of mittens.

Looking for Letter Matches

Directions: Be a detective! Color the magnifying glasses that have the matching uppercase and lowercase letters.

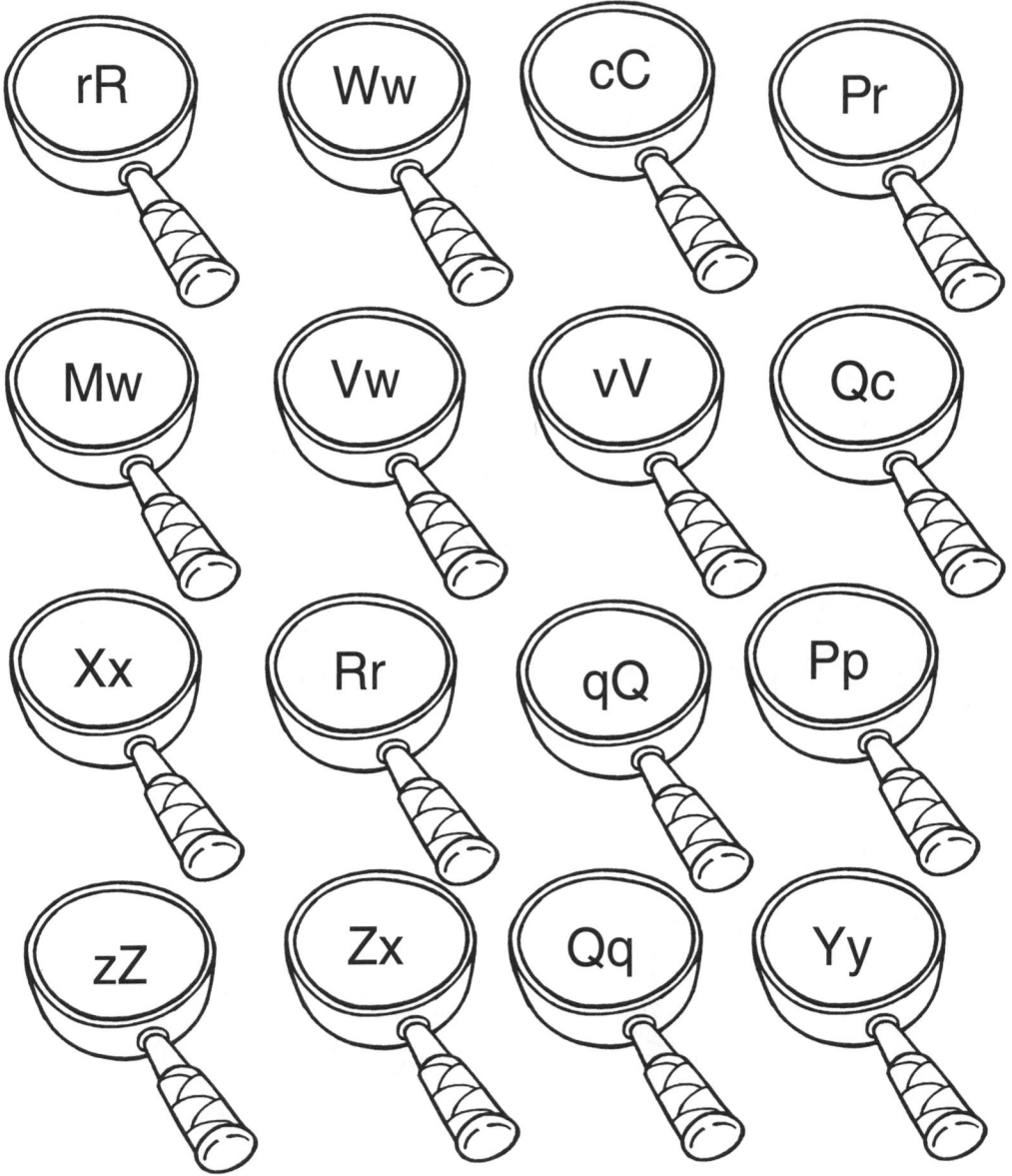

What Do You See?

Directions: Color every space with an **A** red. Color every space with an **a** green.

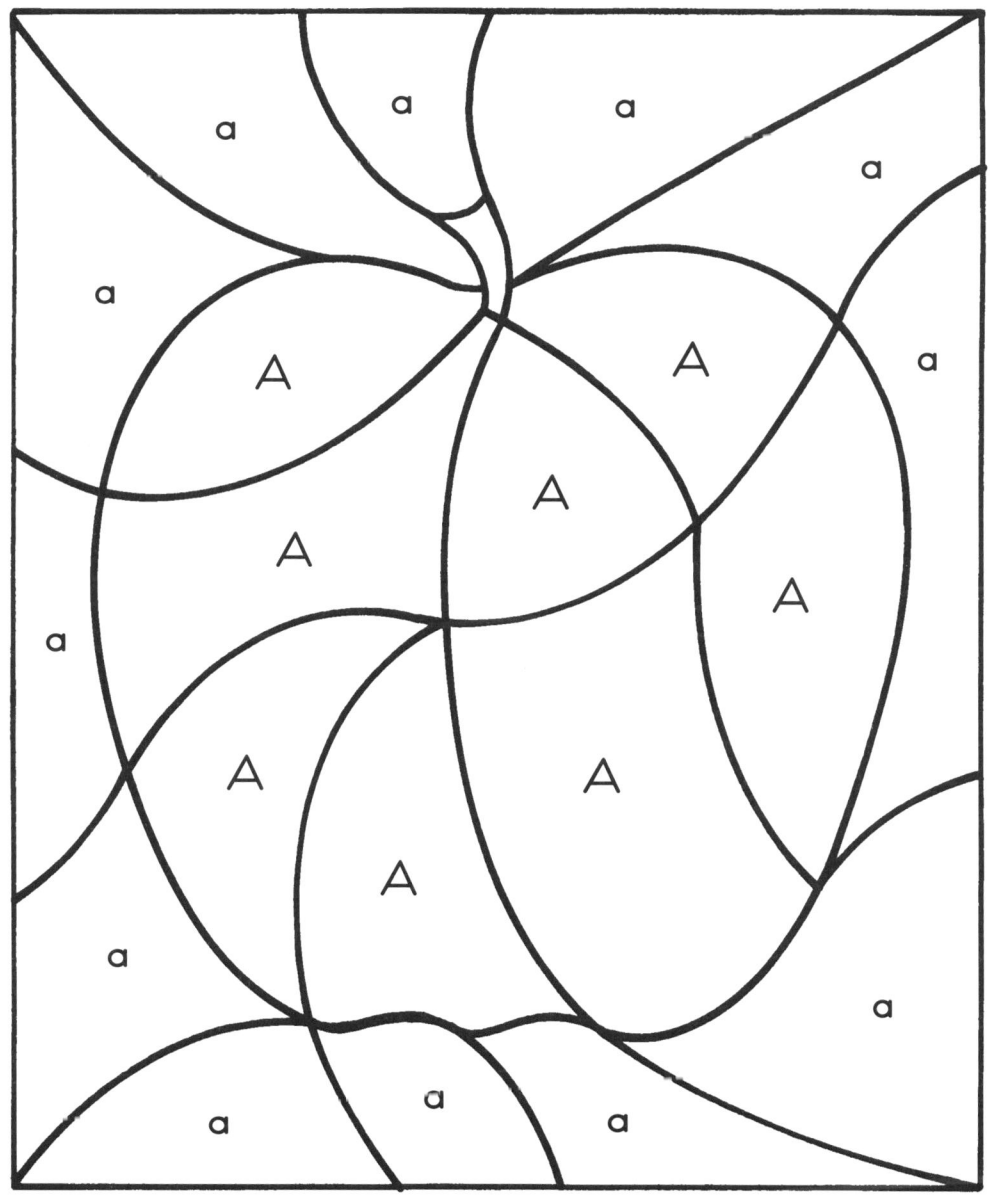

Alphabet Train

Directions: Connect the dots in order from A–Z. Color the picture.

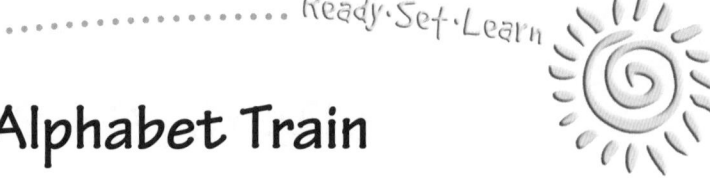

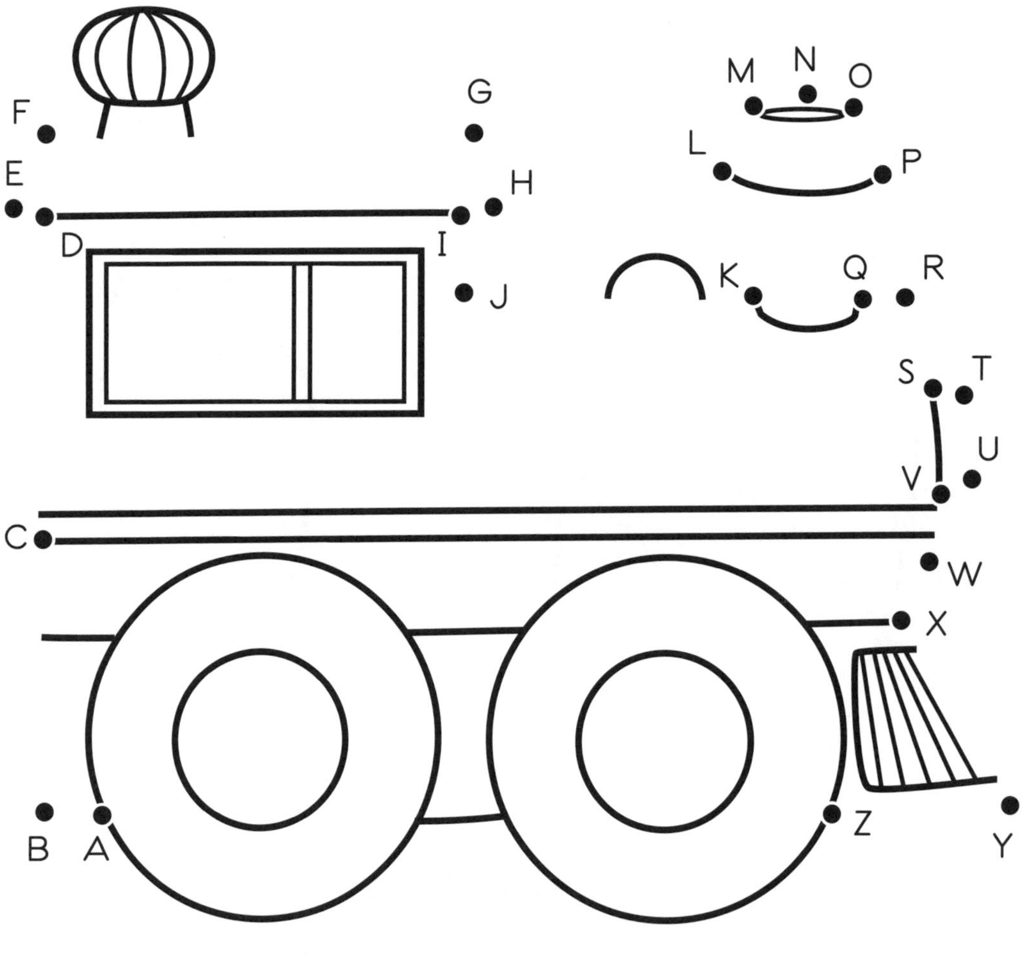

Alphabet Clown

Directions: Connect the dots in order from a–z. Color the picture.

Word Practice

Directions: Write the words on the lines. Color the pictures.

boy

girl

cat

dog

bee

More Word Practice

Directions: Write the words on the lines. Color the pictures.

car

hat

tree

sun

moon

Name Practice

Directions: Write the names on the lines.

Sarah

Jack

Kate

Mrs. Smith

Mr. Chang

Dr. Shaw

Days of the Week

Directions: Write the words on the lines.

Sunday

Monday

Tuesday

Wednesday

Thursday

Friday

Saturday

Sentence Practice

Directions: Write the sentences on the lines.

Today is Monday.

I can ride a bike.

My teacher is Mrs. Smith.

Ready·Set·Learn

This Award Is Presented To

_____

for

★ Doing Your Best

★ Trying Hard

★ Not Giving Up

★ Making a Great Effort